Dedication:
For the gentle hearts,
the curious minds,
and the stars still finding
their glow.
May you always remember—
you belong,
exactly as you are.

In a quiet corner of the universe, tucked between a purple nebula and a giggling cluster of newborn stars, lived a tiny light named Lumi.

Lumi wasn't the biggest star. She wasn't the loudest star.

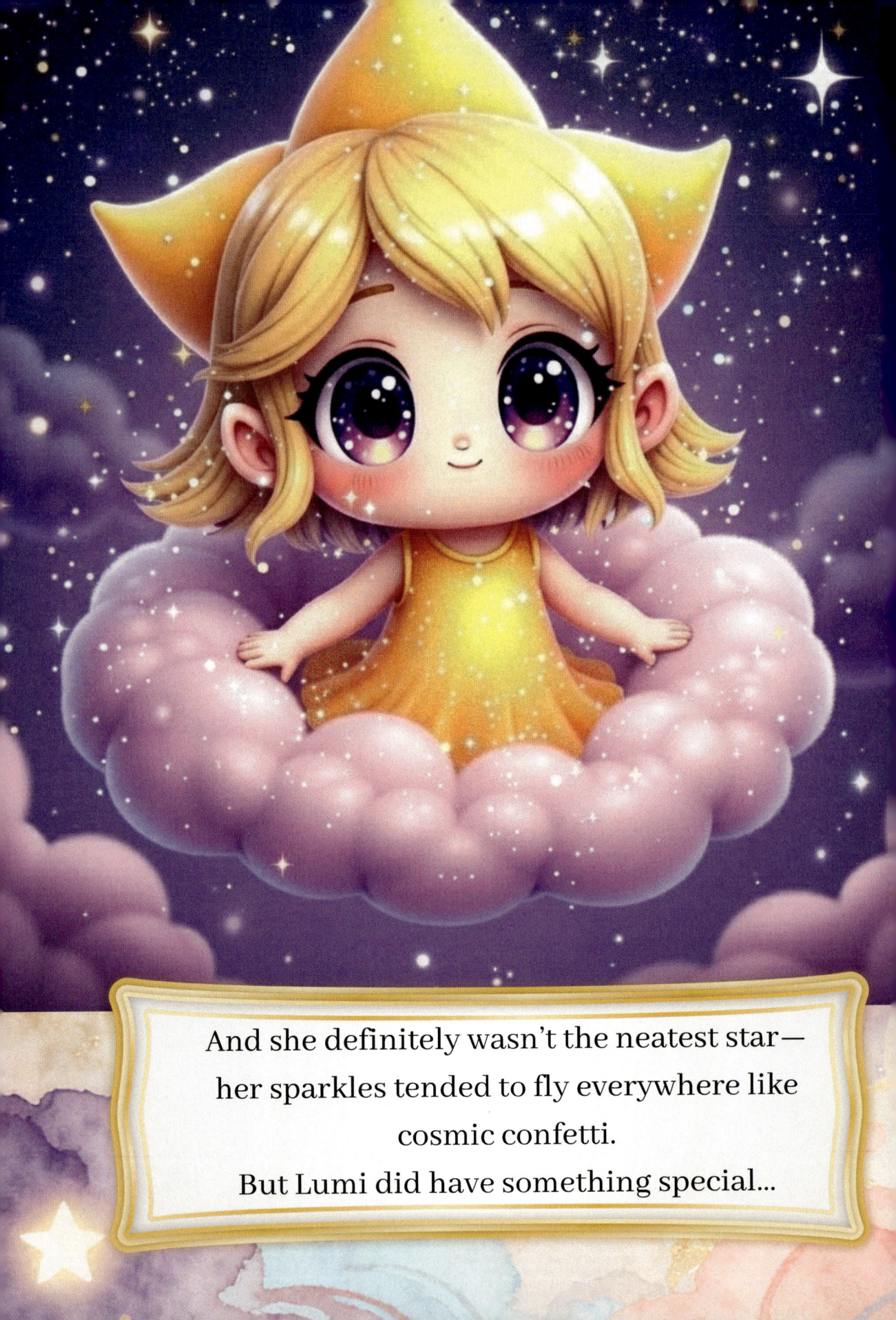

And she definitely wasn't the neatest star—her sparkles tended to fly everywhere like cosmic confetti.
But Lumi did have something special…

She was cosmical,
she was divine,
and she always seemed to be right in line with the
magic of the universe... even when she didn't know it.

One day, Star Teacher Nova gathered all the young stars.
"Today is the Great Galaxy Parade!" Nova announced.

"Every star will shine in a perfect line across the sky!"
All the baby stars cheered... except Lumi.

Lumi's glow flickered nervously. "What if I shine wrong? What if my sparkles get messy? What if I'm not supposed to be in the line at all?"

But Star Teacher Nova bent down and tapped Lumi's glow.

"Little star," she whispered, "when you remember that you are cosmical and divine, your place will always find you."

Lumi wasn't sure what that meant...
but she floated into the parade anyway.

The parade began.
Stars shimmered in a smooth sparkling stream.
Lumi tried to slide into place...

...but she wobbled left.
Then wiggled right.
Then accidentally booped a comet zooming by.

The line rippled. Stars gasped. Lumi panicked.
"I messed everything up," she whispered, curling her glow small.

But just then...
The universe hummed.

A soft wind of stardust swept through the sky, lifting Lumi gently and setting her right where she needed to be... a spot no other star could fill.

Her light stretched...
her glow brightened...
and she realized...
This place felt exactly right.

When the parade finished, all the stars gathered around Lumi.

"Your sparkles made a rainbow in the sky!" one said.
"You filled the empty space perfectly!" said another.

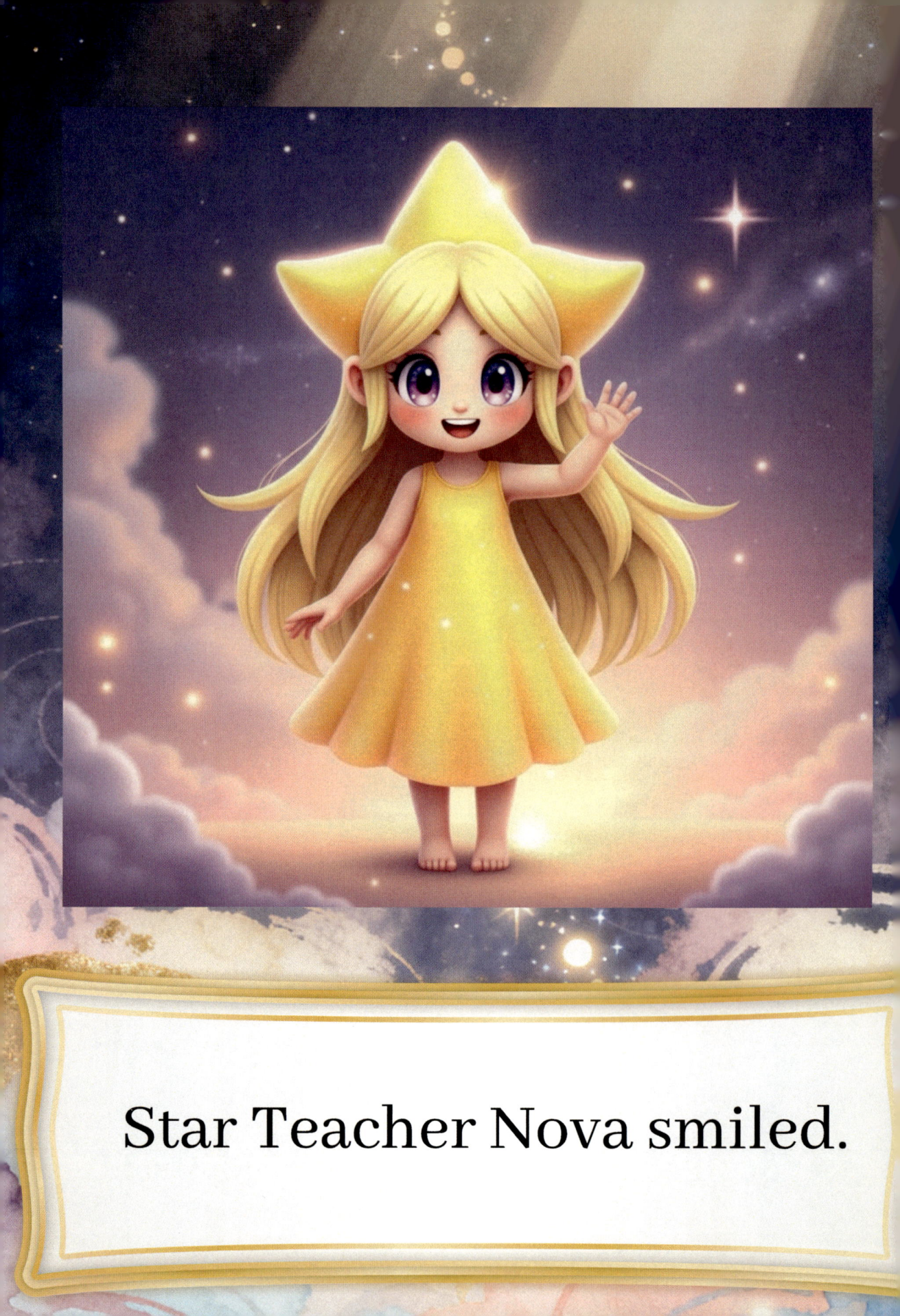

Star Teacher Nova smiled.

"See, Lumi? Being **cosmical** means you're part of everything.

Being **divine** means you **shine** in your own way.

And being in line doesn't mean being perfect…"

She tapped Lumi's glow again. "It means showing up **exactly as you**."

Lumi beamed.... big, bright, beautifully messy.

And from that night on, whenever she felt unsure, she whispered to herself: